WORKING TOWARD ABOLISHING
POVERTY

Tim Cooke

CRABTREE
PUBLISHING COMPANY
WWW.CRABTREEBOOKS.COM

CRABTREE
PUBLISHING COMPANY
WWW.CRABTREEBOOKS.COM

Author: Tim Cooke
Picture Manager: Sophie Mortimer
Designer: Lynne Lennon
Design Manager: Keith Davis
Children's Publisher: Anne O'Daly
Editorial director: Kathy Middleton
Editor: Janine Deschenes
Proofreader: Wendy Scavuzzo
Print coordinator: Katherine Berti

Copyright © Brown Bear
Books Ltd 2020

Photographs: (t=top, b= bottom, l=left, r=right, c=center)

Front Cover: Alamy: Rupert Rivett (center right); Shutterstock: Aspects and Angles (bottom left); Wikimedia Commons (center left)

Interior: Alamy: Duncan Hale-Sutton 37t, Mark Kerrison 25, Jim West 29t; Feeding Children International: 29b; Library of Congress: 11, 23, 27, 32 Roger Higgins 28; NARA: National Archives at College Park 22; Public Domain: Cornell University Library; The PJ Mode Collection 14, Francis Franklin 9, Gift; Government of France 12, Illustrated London News 15 Jacob Riis 19t, 20 Museum of Modern Art; Jacob Riis 18, J Neish 16, the Leisure Hour in 1904, Fed Barnard 13, V. O. HAMMON PUBLISHING CO. 21; Shutterstock: April Cat 19b, arindambanerjee 43b, Jule Berlin 17c, Sara Carpenter 41, Neeraz Chaturvedi 39, Sabhi Click 4, Everett Collection 8, 10, 30, Geemzeeno 42, Slexis Grimsley 1, Don Huan 7b, Sandeep Jeengar 31, Zoran Karapancev 33, 44, Martchan 34, V Maslova 6, Mortortion Films 7t, photka 37b, rawf8 5, Priya Ranjan-Roul 38, Steve Skjold 43t, Steve Sanchez Photos 36 Travel Stock 24; Toronto Disaster Relief Committee: 40; Wellcome Images: 26; Flickr, Confrontational Media: 35.

Brown Bear Books has made every attempt to contact the copyright holder. If you have any information about omissions, please contact licensing@brownbearbooks.co.uk

Library and Archives Canada Cataloging in Publication

Title: Working toward abolishing poverty / Tim Cooke.
Names: Cooke, Tim, 1961- author.
Description: Series statement: Achieving social change | Includes bibliographical references and index.
Identifiers: Canadiana (print) 20200300504 | Canadiana (print) 20200300512 | Canadiana (ebook) 20200300512 | ISBN 9780778779414 (hardcover) | ISBN 9780778779476 (softcover) | ISBN 9781427125453 (HTML)
Subjects: LCSH: Poverty—Juvenile literature. | LCSH: Social policy—Juvenile literature. | LCSH: Social change—Juvenile literature.
Classification: LCC HC79.P6 C66 2021 | DDC j362.5/561—dc23 | 362.5/561—dc23

Library of Congress Cataloging-in-Publication Data

Names: Cooke, Tim, 1961- author.
Title: Working toward abolishing poverty / Tim Cooke.
Description: New York : Crabtree Publishing Company, 2021. | Series: Achieving social change | Includes bibliographical references and index.
Identifiers: LCCN 2020032444 (print) | LCCN 2020032445 (ebook) | ISBN 9780778779414 (hardcover) | ISBN 9780778779476 (paperback) | ISBN 9781427125453 (ebook)
Subjects: LCSH: Poverty--Juvenile literature. | Social policy--Juvenile literature. | Social change--Juvenile literature.
Classification: LCC HC79.P6 C656 2021 (print) | LCC HC79.P6 (ebook) | DDC 362.5/561--dc23
LC record available at https://lccn.loc.gov/2020032444
LC ebook record available at https://lccn.loc.gov/2020032445

Crabtree Publishing Company
www.crabtreebooks.com   1-800-387-7650

Published in Canada
Crabtree Publishing
616 Welland Ave.
St. Catharines, ON
L2M 5V6

Published in the United States
Crabtree Publishing
347 Fifth Ave
Suite 1402-145
New York, NY 10016

Published by CRABTREE PUBLISHING COMPANY in 2021

Printed in the U.S.A./092020/CG20200810

CONTENTS

INTRODUCTION

In the simplest definition, poverty is the state of being poor. However, some definitions of poverty relate to how much money people have. Other definitions include standard-of-living factors, such as health and education.

Someone living in poverty may be unable to afford food, shelter, clothing, or other essentials. They may be without a job or earn very little and rely on aid from governments or charities. In the worst cases, poverty means they cannot meet their basic needs. Other people are considered poor because they are disadvantaged compared with others in their society. They often work full time, but still have a very low standard of living.

Charities provide food for children living in poverty in India. Food poverty is linked to poor health and low school attendance.

A Question of Standards

One way to measure poverty is to compare living standards. The United Nations (UN) is an international organization that, among other goals, aims to end global poverty. It compares living standards by using the Multidimensional Poverty Index (MPI). The MPI measures 10 indicators linked to people's health, education, and standard of living. According to these indicators, being poor might be reflected in someone not being able to afford good **sanitation** or electricity, for example, or not being able to attend school for long enough to get a full education.

For as long as poverty has existed, people have tried to improve the lives of those living in poverty. However, the problem of poverty is complex. Many experts see poverty as a sign of wider issues. They believe issues such as the quality of education and the availability of opportunities to earn money make it difficult for people to escape poverty.

Poverty is closely linked to social issues such as homelessness and gender inequality. In many places, women find it more difficult to earn money than men, so poverty affects them more.

CHAPTER 1

WHAT IS POVERTY?

Debates about tackling poverty begin with defining the problem. Definitions of poverty are usually developed by governments and international organizations. But these definitions do not always include all people affected by poverty.

Extreme or absolute poverty is the condition in which a person does not make enough money to meet all of their basic needs. It is often measured against how much money someone has to meet these needs. Countries set their own measures, but the most widely used measure was set by the World Health Organization in 2015. It set an international poverty line at $1.90 per day. By this measure, anyone with a lower income lives in extreme poverty.

Relative poverty is measured in different ways. In the United States, for example, someone is below the poverty line if they earn less than 60 percent of the median, or middle, income. In 2018, that was just over $25,000 for a family of two parents and two children.

One way to measure poverty is to compare the cost of food to a person's income.

Poverty is a serious problem for seniors who can no longer earn an income.

Other Measures

Canada uses three measures of poverty. The market basket measure (MBM) compares family income with the cost of a basic lifestyle, including food, clothing, housing, and transportation. Families included in the low-income cut-off (LICO) spend at least 20 percent more of their income on basic needs than other families. In other words, they have less money left after meeting their basic needs. The low income measure (LIM) includes people with less than 50 percent of **median** household income.

How poverty is defined is important. It often decides who receives financial support from the state, in the form of **welfare** such as social security. **Activists** point out that some people who are classified above the poverty line still struggle to make ends meet. Activists push governments to use definitions of poverty that will help as many people as possible.

The History of Poverty

For most of history, poor people were forced to rely on the support of landowners or the church. In hard times, such as poor harvests, many people died from lack of food.

In 1601, a law in England instructed local councils to help poor people by giving them money, food, or clothing. In the late 1700s, society began to change. As factories were built in cities, people moved there from the country to find work. Many people earned better wages, but there were not enough jobs for everyone. Some people who moved to the city to seek high wages became poorer still. As poverty grew, towns could not afford to provide assistance to everyone who was poor. They began to refuse entry to poor newcomers. Towns even hired out poor people to work for citizens who would pay for their support.

Children huddle around steam from a grate as a wealthy family walks by. In industrial cities, wealth and poverty often existed side by side.

Poorhouses like this one in England were purposely made unpleasant to discourage people from moving there. They served poor food and people slept in overcrowded, dirty conditions.

The Poorhouse System

Some places forced people seeking help to live in poorhouses (called workhouses in England). Residents did hard labor in return for basic food and housing, and lived by harsh rules. People who ran poorhouses wanted to force poor people to find other ways to support themselves. Only the most desperate people moved into poorhouses. They were being punished for being poor.

Poor people were often blamed for their poverty. Observers often wrongly made a distinction between the "deserving" poor, who were simply unlucky, and the "undeserving poor," whose poverty was caused by laziness, poor **morals**, or drunkenness.

Viewpoints

As the effects of poverty grew worse in the 1800s, local organizations failed to cope. In Europe, reformers called on governments to help.

At the time, men needed to own property to vote and women could not vote at all, so poor people had no political power. They relied on better-off members of society to help them, either by providing **charity** or by changing the laws to reduce levels of poverty.

In many countries, social reformers pressed governments to improve conditions for poor people. In the 1880s, reformers got the government in Prussia (now Germany) to become the first country to make welfare payments to sick people and elderly people. Other countries followed in the early 1900s. Welfare was funded by making wealthier members of society pay taxes.

Reformers wanted to knock down cramped, poor-quality housing like this. Instead, they wanted to build homes with more space and better sanitation.

Welfare was **controversial**. Critics argued that it added to the problem of poverty. They claimed that giving people money encouraged them not to work. Even some activists who fought to help poor people believed poverty was the result of bad morals. Religious leaders were among those who blamed poor people for their own poverty.

Victims of Economics

Other people saw poverty as the result of an unfair economic system. They argued that anyone could be poor, and that poverty had a **disproportionate** impact on certain groups in society. These groups included unskilled workers, immigrants, women, and children. Modern activists still see gender as playing a key role in poverty, along with factors such as race, level of education, and migration.

The Salvation Army, formed in 1865, believed that raising people out of poverty included teaching them Christian values.

CHAPTER 2

EARLY SOCIAL REFORMERS

For poor people living in dirty, overcrowded areas in central London, a visit from wealthier neighbors was the last straw. It was 1849, and the well-dressed gentlemen had come to complain about the smell of the alleyways in the slum.

One of the few **literate** men in the slum wrote a letter to a newspaper. It said their neighbors "were much surprized to see the seller [cellar] in our lane… and would not believe that sixty persons sleep in it every night." He wrote, "Preaye [pray] Sir com and see us, for we are living like piggs, and it aint faire we shoulde be so ill treted."

The letter was unusual, as it represented the voice of poor people themselves. They usually had to rely on others to speak out for them. One strong voice was the author Charles Dickens.

Dickens walked for miles at night through narrow city streets, seeing how the poorest people lived.

> It is said that the children of the very poor are not brought up, but dragged up.
>
> Charles Dickens

Young Charles Dickens sleeps in a factory where he made shoe polish. Dickens's father had been sent to prison for debt and the family had fallen into poverty.

Writing for Change

Dickens had been raised in poverty. When he was famous, he often visited poor parts of London. He hoped to inspire change by describing in his novels what he saw. In *Oliver Twist*, for example, Dickens described life in a workhouse to try to get the government to close workhouses. Dickens hoped his readers would be so angry after reading about workhouses that they would force politicians to change things.

Dickens also helped poor people in more direct ways. For example, he set up a home for homeless women in London called Urania Cottage.

Conditional Assistance

Many individuals used their privilege or money to help those living in poverty. However, their efforts were often influenced by ideas about who deserved to be helped.

Some activists helped poor people, but believed they needed to change their behavior, too. In 1865, William Booth founded the Christian Mission in England to improve the lives of the poor and to preach Christian values. His organization was renamed the Salvation Army in 1878. Its first American branch opened in Pennsylvania two years later. Church officers fed and housed poor people, while encouraging them to adopt more "moral" attitudes toward life. At the time, many anti-poverty activists believed that low morals encouraged poverty. For example, they wanted to help poor people by making alcohol illegal, or not allowed by law.

The Salvation Army offered the hope of better social conditions for poor people who followed their Christian message.

*In 1869, **philanthropist** Angela Burdette-Coutts built this grand market in a poor part of east London, England, to encourage people to eat fresh food. She was influenced by Charles Dickens.*

Other reformers went further. But some solutions were controversial and morally wrong. The Oregon physician Bethenia Angelina Owens-Adair, for example, argued that one way to get rid of poverty would be to **sterilize** some of the poorest members of society, such as the mentally ill.

Individual Actions

Other activists thought people living in poverty would benefit from better facilities. In England, Mary Carpenter opened free schools to improve education for poor children, while Octavia Hill wanted cities to build parks. Parks would provide clean air and space to relax and walk. Angela Burdette-Coutts used her fortune to provide housing, clean water, and schools in the poorest parts of London.

Key Voices

Josephine Lowell

The wealthy businesswoman Josephine Shaw Lowell became involved in social reform after being widowed during the American Civil War (1861–1865). Among her contributions was creating the Consumers' League of New York City to improve the conditions of poor women workers. She also set up the House of Refuge for Women in New York. However, she argued that very poor people should be sent to workhouses to learn moral values.

Political Moves

Some groups wanted to change poverty through politics. They included trade unions, which claimed rights for workers, and groups calling for more people to be able to vote.

In France, the economist Comte de Saint-Simon argued that the growth of industry would change society. It would give poor people more opportunity to earn money and would teach them about technology. They would become more involved in society. Saint-Simon predicted that this would help to create a "brotherhood of man." His ideas are seen as an early form of **socialism**. Under socialism, the economy is run for the good of the whole community.

As industry grew, some workers formed groups to try to protect their rights. These became the first trade unions.

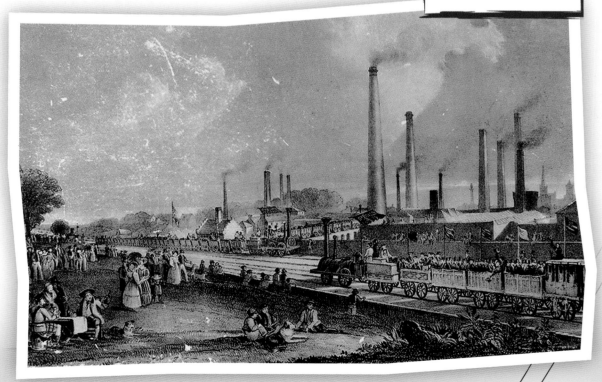

In 1848, similar beliefs inspired the French politician Louis Blanc to set up a system of National Workshops to provide work for unemployed people in France. The system worked well at first, but failed when there were not enough jobs for everyone.

Communism and Wealth Distribution

The conditions of workers in cities in Germany and England, meanwhile, inspired the German economists Karl Marx and Friedrich Engels to suggest a system called **communism** in 1848. They saw that workers did not receive the wealth created by their labor. Instead, it went to business owners. Under communism, workers would run a government that controlled the economy and distributed wealth more fairly.

*Marx (left) and Engels argued that workers should take control of the economy in a **revolution**.*

Key Events

Utopias

Some activists set up utopias, or ideal communities, to avoid social problems. Around 1800, the mill owner Robert Owen built a village for his workers in Scotland (right), with homes and a school. Meanwhile, people in communities such as Oneida in New York or Amana in Iowa shared their property, so no one was better off than anyone else.

CHAPTER 3

THE EARLY 1900S

The terrible conditions he saw made Jacob Riis feel sick. Born in Denmark, Riis came to New York City in 1870 and became a police reporter. Shocked by the city's poverty, Riis began to photograph the slums of Manhattan.

Riis visited places few people had ever seen, including the city's most **notorious** neighborhoods. He wanted to make his readers aware of the terrible conditions there. He published his images in 1889. They helped persuade the city council to rebuild the worst slums. Riis is now seen as one of the major forces behind reform in New York.

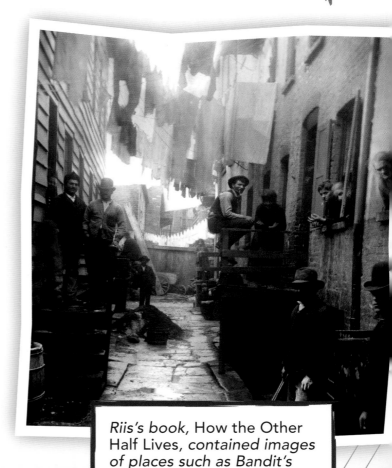

Oh God! That bread should be so dear, and flesh and blood so cheap.

Jacob Riis

Riis's book, How the Other Half Lives, *contained images of places such as Bandit's Roost, shown here, a center of criminal activity.*

Riis photographed children sleeping in an alleyway. Some children had never been farther than five minutes from where they lived.

Raking Muck

Riis was one of the "**Muckrakers**" who highlighted issues in American society during the Progressive Era, from about 1890 to 1920. The writer Upton Sinclair, for example, described the harsh conditions in the meatpacking industry in Chicago. His book, *The Jungle*, led to the United States government introducing laws to improve food safety, including federal inspections of meat-processing factories.

The Muckrakers were inspired by *Progress and Poverty*, an 1879 book by the economist Henry George. George wondered why desperate poverty accompanied economic growth in the United States. He argued that wealth generated by land and **natural resources** should belong equally to all members of society. His ideas influenced anti-poverty campaigners in the Progressive Era and beyond.

A Growing Voice

At the start of the 1900s, many activists tried to help people in urban poverty. In North America, Protestant teachings inspired a form of activism called the Social Gospel.

The Social Gospel promoted the idea that the church should improve the lives of the poor. One of its creators, Walter Rauschenbusch, wanted the church to help improve slums, reduce alcohol addiction, and improve economic equality.

The Social Gospel inspired the settlement house movement, in which activists set up bases in American cities. Settlement houses acted as centers providing education, medical care, and food for people in poor neighborhoods. By 1920, there were about 500 settlement houses in the United States.

Walter Rauschenbusch was a pastor in Hell's Kitchen, a poor area in Manhattan.

Hull-House

Hull-House was founded by Jane Addams and Ellen Gates Starr in 1889 to help poor immigrants on Chicago's West Side. The organization mapped the income of individual streets to show where poverty was worst. It pushed local authorities into housing reform and other practical measures. Florence Kelley, who worked at Hull-House, investigated the conditions of poor immigrants who worked in **sweatshops**. In 1893, her work led Illinois to adopt its first laws for the protection of workers.

By 1912, Hull-House had expanded to include 13 buildings in Chicago and a summer camp outside the city.

Key Voices

Catherine Doherty

In 1932, the Russian-born Canadian Catherine Doherty gave up her possessions and moved to live with the homeless in Toronto, Canada. This was similar to actions made by monks and nuns in the past. She used donations to set up Friendship House to provide food for the poor, together with Catholic education. She went on to create a similar organization in Harlem, New York.

The Great Depression

The Great Depression that began in 1929 plunged millions of people into poverty as economic activity slowed, businesses closed, and unemployment rose massively.

Millions of men were out of work. The young Canadian Tommy Douglas, studying in Chicago, witnessed the conditions in the city's homeless camps. Influenced by the Social Gospel movement, Douglas came to the conclusion that poverty should be fought with practical measures. When Douglas later became a politician in Saskatchewan, for example, he introduced Canada's first public health care system.

Unemployed people relied on soup kitchens for food. One soup kitchen in Chicago was even set up by the gangster Al Capone.

The New Deal

In 1933, the U.S. administration of Franklin D. Roosevelt introduced the New Deal. This was a program of measures motivated by a desire to create work so that workers would spend their pay and kick-start the economy. Poverty levels remained high, however. Photographer Dorothea Lange created a famous image of poverty in 1936. *Migrant Mother* shows a woman and her children seeking farm work in California, after drought had ruined farms in the Midwest. In 1935, Roosevelt introduced the first U.S. welfare measure, the Social Security Act. It introduced pensions that reduced poverty among the old-age population, and provided benefits for the unemployed and the sick.

Florence Owens Thompson, pictured in the famous photo, was 32 years old and had seven children when Dorothea Lange photographed Migrant Mother.

Key Events

On-to-Ottawa Trek

In Canada, poor workers spoke for themselves in the 1935 On-to-Ottawa Trek. About 1,000 unemployed men left British Columbia by train for Ottawa to complain about the camps where they lived. In Regina, Saskatchewan, the police broke up a rally by the workers. A riot began that left two men dead. Preventing such outbreaks of violence was one motivation for governments to create relief programs.

CHAPTER 4

YOUTH AND POVERTY

London schoolgirl Amika George could not believe the magazine article she was reading. Throughout the UK, she learned, one in ten young women could not afford sanitary products during their periods.

Women used newspaper instead of tampons, or stayed off school one week a month. Amika learned that some girls' families had to choose between buying sanitary products and buying food. In 2017, Amika founded Free Periods, a group that wanted free sanitary products in all UK schools. Despite facing online bullies, Amika collected more than 27,000 signatures on a petition, or formal written request, urging government action.

*Girls in countries all over the world miss a large part of their education because **period poverty** keeps them away from school.*

If you feel that something has to change, be the person to start that change.

Amika George

In 2019, the government agreed that schools would provide free sanitary products. Amika's campaign continued, however. Sanitary products in Britain, many American states, and elsewhere were taxed as **luxuries**. Amika wanted them classed as necessities, so the tax is reduced or removed.

Youth Activism

Amika George is just one of a number of young activists addressing poverty. Poverty is a particular issue for young people, because children suffer its effects disproportionately. They suffer more from a poor diet, for example, and are less able than adults to earn money. Activists targeted child poverty from early in the anti-poverty movement.

Save the Children

In 1870, Dr. Thomas John Barnardo opened his first home for orphans in London. When he died 35 years later, more than 8,500 children lived in Barnardo's homes.

Barnardo accepted children seen as being "undeserving" and cared for neglected groups, such as disabled children. Barnardo was also controversial. He took children from their parents without permission. His homes later sent 150,000 children to British **colonies**, mainly Australia and Canada, where many were forced into hard labor.

This image shows a class of Barnardo's boys in east London. Barnardo was accused 88 times of taking children from their parents. He argued this was necessary to help the children.

Key Events

Declaration of the Rights of the Child

Eglantyne Jebb's Declaration of the Rights of the Child was adopted by the League of Nations in 1924. In 1959, it was expanded and adopted by the United Nations. The document promotes children's rights around the world. Among the rights it claims for children is the right to be helped first in times of distress, such as periods of poverty.

Lewis Wickes Hine photographed children working in cotton mills surrounded by dangerous spinning machines.

Save the Children

World War I (1914–1918) left many people in desperate poverty in central Europe. In 1919, the wealthy British sisters Eglantyne Jebb and Dorothy Buxton raised money to help poor European children. Their success led them to found Save the Children, which in 1924 drafted the Declaration of the Rights of the Child. This declaration formed the basis of international anti-child-poverty campaigning for much of the 1900s.

Ending Child Labor

In the United States, meanwhile, the photographer Lewis Wickes Hine was one of the Muckrakers of the Progressive Era. Working for the National Child Labor Committee, Hine photographed child workers in cotton mills and other locations in a campaign that eventually led in 1938 to the **abolition** of child labor in the United States.

Continuing Efforts

During the civil rights movement in the 1960s in the United States, activists fought for equal political rights for Black Americans. They also highlighted the disproportionate levels of poverty faced by Black communities.

Individual activists used different tactics to tackle the problem of poverty in Black communities. Shirley Chisholm, an educator in Brooklyn in the 1950s, was convinced that education in early years was key to helping children escape poverty. Chisholm was elected to the New York State Assembly, and in 1968 to the U.S. Congress.

Marian Wright Edelman, a Mississippi lawyer, worked with low-income families for the Poor People's Campaign, an anti-poverty initiative that aimed to influence government policies and empower the poor. In 1973, Edelman began the Children's Defense Fund to coordinate efforts to help poor children.

In Congress, Shirley Chisholm helped expand the food stamp program that provided milk and food for babies and their mothers.

Today, the Children's Defense Fund carries out careful **statistical** research into poverty. It uses the evidence to figure out what new laws would most improve the lives of poor children.

Fighting Poverty

In 2017, 13 million American children still lived in poverty. Black children were three times as likely as White children to live in poverty. Groups such as the Children's Defense Fund and the U.S. Child Poverty Action Group are trying to force the U.S. government to establish a national **strategy**. They want to set a target to reduce child poverty to half within 10 years and eliminate it within 20 years.

Around one in three Black children in the United States live in poverty. For all American children, the figure is around one in six.

Fighting Child Hunger

Former U.S. Marine Richard Proudfit was inspired to found a charity to feed poor children after volunteering in Honduras after a hurricane in 1974. Kids Against Hunger had sent more than 2 billion meals around the world by the time Proudfit died in 2018.

CHAPTER 5

THE LATER 20TH CENTURY

Most days, Lotta Hitschmanova got home to eat around 6:00 p.m. An hour later, she was back in her office at 56 Sparks Street, Ottawa, to work until midnight.

She only broke her routine when she was traveling to check the projects funded by the Unitarian Service Committee of Canada (USC). She began the organization to look after homeless children after World War II (1939–1945), but it expanded to help the poor around the world, focusing on the Middle East and Asia. With donations from more than 500,000 Canadians, Hitschmanova worked constantly to improve the lives of poor people.

> The need...
> is immense,
> unimaginable,
> and we should be
> doing much more.
> Lotta Hitschmanova

At the end of World War II in 1945, many Europeans were left without homes or resources.

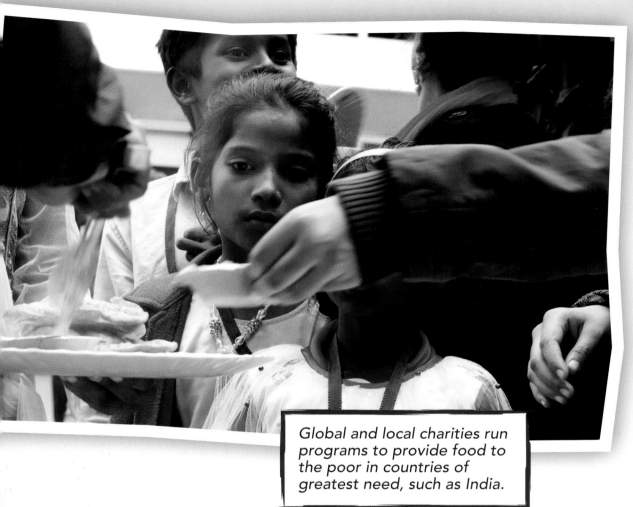

Global and local charities run programs to provide food to the poor in countries of greatest need, such as India.

Global Activism

Hitschmanova argued that charities should work where the need was greatest. In the second half of the 20th century, anti-poverty activism more generally began to focus on global rather than **domestic** poverty.

Large-scale organizations such as Tearfund and the UK charity Christian Aid began to help poor people in places such as Africa and Asia. The relative need was greater there than at home, where welfare systems had reduced levels of extreme poverty. In addition, activists were beginning to understand that poverty everywhere was connected. International migration meant that poverty was forcing people to move from their homes to other countries.

Direct Action

Despite the growing focus on tackling global poverty, some activists still concentrated on fighting poverty at home. They tried to convince governments to support poor people better.

These activists included the civil rights leader Martin Luther King, Jr. He founded the Poor People's Campaign in 1968, shortly before his **assassination**, to help Americans out of poverty. In 1964, U.S. president Lyndon B. Johnson had announced a War on Poverty that had lifted millions of Americans above the poverty line, but there were still 23 million poor. They included a disproportionate number of Black Americans. In May and June 1968, more than 3,000 protestors occupied a camp on the National Mall in Washington, DC, calling for full employment, higher incomes, and better housing.

Marchers protest poverty in Washington, DC, in June 1968. Martin Luther King, Jr. had been assassinated on April 4.

Action in Ontario

In 1990, Canadian activists formed the Ontario Coalition Against Poverty (OCAP) to take **direct action** to help shape government policy. At a time when the authorities were reducing welfare provision, OCAP organized collective action, including **squatting** in empty buildings and setting up a tent city in a local park. When 1,000 people marched on the Ontario government building to support the homeless, the police charged the peaceful protestors on horses, with dozens of injuries and arrests.

Gaeten Heroux, an activist with OCAP, speaks during protests against a meeting of the world's richest nations in Toronto in 2010.

Key Voices

Civil Rights Leader

In 1967, Martin Luther King, Jr., outlined his view that government attempts to fix individual causes of poverty, such as low-quality housing or bad education, were misplaced. King proposed instead that the government should provide everyone with a certain income. Some poverty activists today still support the idea of a **universal basic income**.

Vulnerable Groups

In the late 20th century, some activists explored the connection between poverty and vulnerable, or at-risk, and disadvantaged groups in society. These groups include women and Indigenous peoples.

Women are more likely than men to be victims of poverty, so anti-poverty activism is closely linked to gender equality. The charity ONE runs a campaign called Poverty is Sexist. It explains how poverty worsens the effects of **sexism**. Fewer women work than men, and they are paid about 24 percent less. Women's jobs are also often less secure than those of men. Many women are also responsible for unpaid work, such as cleaning, cooking, and childcare in the home. About 130 million girls cannot access the level of education that might lift them out of poverty. Many can be forced into marriages.

In countries such as Ethiopia, women suffer more from poverty because they spend much of their time on unpaid tasks such as collecting water.

*The American Indian Movement (AIM) uses tactics such as protests to address **systemic** poverty in Indigenous communities in the United States.*

Indigenous Peoples

Poverty is damaging for many Indigenous peoples. Although Indigenous peoples make up 5 percent of the global population, they account for about 15 percent of the world's extreme poor. Groups such as the Métis of Canada formed political associations in the 1940s and 1950s to gain economic support. In 2010, the Poverty Action Research Project was created to study poverty among five First Nations. It recommended, for example, developing business leadership among First Nations communities.

In Australia, **Aboriginal** communities face poverty and low standards of living. Nearly 20 percent of Aboriginal peoples there live in poverty, and more than one-third have experienced being homeless. Charities work with Aboriginal peoples to create economic opportunities. Led by Aboriginal Australians, for example, Caritas began a program in the Tjanpi Desert to encourage women in remote communities to create and sell baskets, beads, and fiber art. This also helps preserve and celebrate their culture.

CHAPTER 6

CAMPAIGNING AGAINST POVERTY TODAY

By the 2010s, many governments were alarmed by the cost of welfare. Some attempted to reduce costs by cutting the services they provided. Poor people were again left relying for help on charity rather than the state.

In the face of welfare cuts in the United States, the Reverend William Barber II resurrected the 1968 Poor People's Campaign in 2018. Thousands of people marched in Washington, DC, to demand better wages. The marchers included groups such as Fight for $15, which called for a raise in the federal minimum wage to $15 an hour from the $7.25 set in 2007. Some states and cities did eventually raise local minimum wages. In June 2020, a further march against poverty took place digitally during the COVID-19 pandemic. Thousands of participants logged on to take part.

An activist takes the message of the Poor People's Campaign into Wall Street, in the heart of New York's financial district.

Everybody's Got a Right to Live

GET WALL STREET OUT OF OUR HEALTHCARE #SINGLEPAYERNow #PassNYHe

> Overcoming poverty is not a gesture of charity, but an act of justice.
> Nelson Mandela

In the Make Poverty History march in 2005, more than 36 million people in 70 countries called for help for the world's poorest countries.

Rights and Responsibilities

Meanwhile, Indigenous peoples from North and South America spoke up to protect their economic rights throughout the continent. Canadian Obijwe activist Rodney Bobiwash shared his experience with other Indigenous peoples. He helped ensure they had representatives in the decision-making processes of organizations such as the World Bank or the Organization for American States (OAS). He was also a voice for anti-racism, education for Indigenous peoples, and expanded support and services for Indigenous university students.

Key Events

Sustainable Development Goals

In 2000, world leaders at the United Nations agreed to the Millennium Declaration. This agreement committed members of the UN to a series of interlinked goals aimed at lifting all countries out of poverty. In 2015, the commitment was updated to create the UN's Sustainable Development Goals. The first goal is to end poverty in all its forms.

Power to the Poor

In the contemporary world, activism takes many forms. Some activists have come up with a new economic model. This approach sets out to empower the poor to earn money.

The Grameen Bank was founded by Bangladeshi banker Muhammad Yunus in 1983. Realizing that a small amount of money could make a difference, he came up with the idea of **microfinancing**. The bank made tiny loans to people who were too poor to get a loan from a regular bank. This allowed people to buy materials or tools to start their own businesses.

A microloan to buy cane can enable someone to start a business weaving baskets to sell to their neighbors.

Key Voices

Hondurans Help Hondurans

In 1993, women from poor farming communities in Honduras founded COMUCAP to stop violence against women. COMUCAP soon shifted its focus to poverty. It taught women to grow and sell organic coffee and aloe vera, giving them economic independence. It now provides jobs and incomes for more than 250 women, often from abusive homes.

A group of Indian women apply for a microloan from a bank worker. Without access to education, many such women cannot write, so they sign contracts with their fingerprints.

In Nigeria, meanwhile, Abisoye Ajayi-Akinfolarin founded the Pearls Africa Foundation to teach coding to girls from one of Nigeria's biggest slums. The foundation has given hundreds of young women the technical skills to work their way out of poverty.

Standing up for Their Community

In North America, too, activists are fighting poverty in their own communities, often as part of a wider campaign including land rights and environmental activism. The Thunder Valley Community Development Corporation in South Dakota, for example, was formed to reduce dependence on fossil fuel industries but also to improve housing and create a reliable supply of food. The youth activist Jasilyn Charger of the Cheyenne River Sioux Tribe set up mental-health support for Native American teens before helping to found the International Indigenous Youth Council. This group encourages young people to improve conditions in their communities.

Changemakers

As high costs and political choices lead governments to reduce provisions for poor people, organizations and individual activists keep the defeat of poverty in public focus.

Some organizations, such as the Children's Defense Fund in the United States and the Joseph Rowntree Foundation in the UK concentrate on using data to change public policy about poverty. Among the aims of the Joseph Rowntree Foundation, for example, are ensuring the availability of childcare and affordable transportation so that people can work more easily.

Many individuals and other groups focus instead on trying to ease the effects of poverty. Feeding America, the national food bank network in the United States, fed 4.3 billion meals to 40 million Americans in 2018.

In Britain, the Trussell Trust runs food banks but also encourages politicians and public bodies to address the causes of poverty.

Street nurse Cathy Crowe trained as a nurse before becoming involved in issues surrounding poverty.

Key Voices

Care on the Streets

Cathy Crowe is a "street nurse" who began to help homeless people in Toronto, Canada, in the 1990s. Crowe also fights for better housing for poor people. She wants all levels of government to increase their spending on social housing by one percent. Street nurses also operate in other Canadian cities.

A New Threat

Activists feared that the 2020 global **pandemic** of COVID-19 would bring a new threat to those living in poverty. More than 55 percent of the world's population had no welfare protection from the economic fallout of the pandemic, as small businesses closed their doors and unemployment rose. In many countries, **mutual-aid groups** formed to take on tasks such as distributing food to people who needed it most or giving face masks to homeless people.

Private groups such as churches often organize food banks that provide necessities directly to poor members of communities.

GET INVOLVED

There are many forms of activism against poverty. They range from daily actions to becoming involved in campaigns.

1 Donate

You could make a contribution by donating clothes or food to a local charity. You could also raise money for charities by organizing events such as yard sales.

100% CHARITY
FOR INFORMATION VISIT
WWW.STEPSRECOVERY.COM
OR CALL 905-762-4551

STEPS
905-508-0300
ALL DONATED ITEMS
MUST FIT IN BIN
NO MATTRESSES-FURNITURE-APPLIANCES
Pick-Up Mon-Sun 8am to 5pm

2 Be Informed

The more you know about the fight against poverty, the better you can share that information with other people to convince them to join in. Activist organizations post regular updates of what they've been doing and their future plans.

3 Raise Awareness

Keep the problem of poverty on the agenda by writing to your elected representatives. Alternatively, support a charity such as Dignity for All. Its members send thousands of postcards urging Canadian policymakers to make ending poverty a key government goal.

4 Volunteer

Charities always need volunteers to help raise money and publicize their work. Kids Against Hunger in the United States, for example, relies upon volunteers to pack boxes with thousands of dried meals for distribution around the world.

5 March!

You can show your determination to help end poverty by joining marches and other public demonstrations. The International Day for the Eradication of Poverty is held every October. Check online to find out what events are planned for your area—and if nothing is planned, why not organize something yourself?

Timeline

1834 The Poor Law Amendment Act introduces workhouses in the United Kingdom.

1838 Charles Dickens describes conditions in workhouses in *Oliver Twist*.

1848 Louis Blanc sets up a system of National Workshops to employ the poor in France.

1848 Karl Marx and Freidrich Engels write *The Communist Manifesto*.

1879 Economist Henry George writes an influential study called *Progress and Poverty*.

1889 Germany introduces the world's first welfare system to look after poor groups in society.

1889 Hull-House opens in Chicago, where it becomes a center of anti-poverty activity among poor immigrants.

1924 Influenced by Save the Children, the League of Nations adopts the Declaration of the Rights of the Child.

1929 The Great Depression begins in the United States and spreads to much of the world.

1935 The On-to-Ottawa Trek in Canada ends in violent clashes between unemployed men and the police.

1945 Former refugee Lotta Hitschmanova founds the Unitarian Service Committee of Canada.

1968 The Poor People's Campaign in the United States calls for improved equality in society.

1983 Grameen Bank is founded in Bangladesh, beginning the use of "microfinancing" to help the poor.

2005 A global day of action, Make Poverty History, achieves major promises of help for poor countries.

2015 The United Nations adopts the Sustainable Development Goals; the first goal is the abolition of poverty.

2018 William Barber II founds a new version of the Poor People's Campaign in the United States.

2020 The economic effects of the COVID-19 pandemic threaten to lead to a rise in global poverty.

Sources

Chapter 1

Allen, Sarah K. "The History of the Poorhouse." Primary Research. primaryresearch.org/the-history-of-the-poorhouse

Mack, Joanna. "How poor is too poor?" Poverty and Social Exclusion. 2016. www.poverty.ac.uk/definitions-poverty

Scott, Katherine. "Making Sense of Poverty Measures." Citizens for Public Justice. October 9, 2014. cpj.ca/making-sense-poverty-measures

Chapter 2

Johnstone, Jennifer. "Charles Dickens & Poverty– And what he might think of Britain today." *History is Now Magazine*. April 13, 2014. https://bit.ly/2DugdLw

"Louis Blanc, 1811–1882." The History of Economic Thought. www.hetwebsite.net/het/profiles/blanc.htm

Ward, Jean M. "Bethenia Owens-Adair (1840–1926)." *The Oregon Encyclopedia*. March 17, 2018. https://bit.ly/33zP5FU

Chapter 3

Bateman, Bradley W. "The Social Gospel and the Progressive Era." National Humanities Center. https://bit.ly/3fyn0RE

Howard, Victor. "On to Ottawa Trek." *The Canadian Encyclopedia*. July 26, 2016. www.thecanadianencyclopedia.ca/en/article/on-to-ottawa-trek

Siegel, Robert. "Jacob Riis: Shedding Light on NYC's 'Other Half.'" NPR. June 30, 2008. www.npr.org/templates/story/story.php?storyId=91981589

Chapter 4

Oppenheim, Maya. "How one teenager's period poverty campaign has sparked change for schoolgirls across Britain." *The Independent*. January 15, 2020. https://bit.ly/3gB535Z

"The photos that changed America: celebrating the work of Lewis Hine." *The Guardian*. February 15, 2018. https://bit.ly/2Xu9ckT

Chapter 5

"About Us." Ontario Coalition Against Poverty. https://ocap.ca/about

Llewellyn, Joyce Thierry. "Lotta Hitschmanova: Canada's 'Mother Teresa' with attitude." Facts and Opinions. December 2014. https://bit.ly/3kkXuTd

Chapter 6

Lovett, Adrian. "Make poverty history? A decade on from Gleneagles, it is a genuine possibility." *The Guardian*. July 6, 2015. https://bit.ly/3gATU5c

Glossary

abolition The formal ending of something

Aboriginal Relating to the Indigenous, or first, peoples of Australia

activists People who work to cause social change

assassination A murder carried out for a political reason

charity Voluntary giving of help or money to those in need; an organization that raises money to help a particular cause

colonies Areas that are governed by another country

communism A political system in which the state controls the economy and distributes wealth equally

controversial Causing high levels of disagreement

direct action The use of public protest rather than negotiations to achieve a particular goal

disadvantaged Having unfavorable circumstances or fewer opportunities for success

disproportionate Having a much larger effect on one group in comparison with an effect on another group

domestic Related to one's own nation rather than other countries

literate Able to read and write

luxuries Items that are not necessary but that are desirable, and often expensive

median The middle number in a group

microfinancing The lending of small amounts of money at low interest rates to encourage business

morals Standards of good behavior

Muckrakers Activists in the early 1900s who exposed unfairness in American society

mutual-aid groups Groups of people who cooperate to help one another

natural resources Materials in nature that can be used for economic gain

notorious Well known for a bad quality

pandemic An outbreak of a disease that covers a large area

period poverty The state of being unable to afford sanitary products

philanthropist A person who donates money to promote the welfare of others

relative In comparison to something else

revolution The overthrow of a government to create a new system

sanitation The provision of clean water and sewage disposal

sexism Discrimination against women on the grounds of their gender

socialism A political system in which workers control and benefit from business

squatting Occupying empty buildings

standard of living The degree of wealth or material comfort someone has

statistical Based on numerical data

sterilize To make it impossible for someone to have children

strategy An overall plan for how to achieve a long-term goal

sweatshops Places where workers are employed for long hours in poor conditions for very low pay

systemic Relating to a system such as education or health care; people living in poverty often have fewer opportunities in these systems

universal basic income A program under which a government would pay everyone in a country enough to live comfortably

welfare Government programs to support people in need

Further Information

Books

Axelrod-Contrada, Joan, and Erin L. McCoy. *Poverty: Public Crisis or Private Struggle?* (Today's Debates). Cavendish Square Publishing, 2019.

Burgan, Michael. *Exposing Hidden Worlds: How Jacob Riis's Photos Became Tools for Social Reform* (Captured History). Compass Point Books, 2017.

Kjelle, Marylou Morano. *The Quest to End World Hunger* (Charity & Philanthropy Unleashed). Mitchell Lane Publishers, 2014.

Senter, Jacqueline Conciatore. *The Muckrakers and Progressive Reformers* (The Fourth Estate: Journalism in North America). Cavendish Square Publishing, 2019.

Sharif, Meghan. *Poverty and Economic Equality* (Hot Topics). Lucent Books, 2018.

Sjonger, Rebecca. *Taking Action to End Poverty* (UN Sustainable Development Goals). Crabtree Publishing Company, 2019.

Websites

cepr.shorthandstories.com/history-poverty
A history of global poverty from the Center for Economic and Policy Research, with many graphs.

www.feedingamerica.org/hunger-in-america
Feeding America's introduction to the problem of poverty in the United States today.

www.hullhousemuseum.org/about-jane-addams
A page from the Hull-House Museum about Jane Addams and the work of the famous settlement house in Chicago.

www.loc.gov/teachers/classroommaterials/themes/great-depression/exhibitions.html
An index of online exhibitions at the Library of Congress related to the Great Depression.

www.unwomen.org/en/news/stories/2019/10/i-am-generation-equality-amika-george-period-poverty
An interview with Amika George from UN Women.

weseedchange.org/lottas-life/
A biography of Lotta Hitschmanova from SeedChange, which was formerly the Unitarian Service Committee.

Index